AI

And

FREELANCE

Create your own

BUSINESS

ONLINE

*Crafty Ink **Manolo***

INDEX

INTRODUCTION

If you dream of working from home, from a beach or anywhere else you like, if you want to have more flexibility, autonomy and creativity in your work, if you want to access a wide range of professional opportunities around the world, then this book and for you.

In this book we will show you how to make money working online with artificial intelligence (AI). This technology that is concerned with creating systems capable of performing tasks that normally require human intelligence, such as image recognition, natural language understanding, problem solving, machine learning and so on. AI is already present in many areas of our daily lives, such as smartphone apps, search engines, social media, streaming services, smart devices and much more.

AI can be a precious ally for your online work, because it can help you:

- Find the online job opportunities that best suit you and your professional goal •
Create and manage your online profile in an effective and captivating
way • Improve your skills and training in a continuous and personalized way • Create
a network of contacts and of employees worldwide • Tackle the challenges and risks of working online safely and responsibly

In this book we will explain what AI is and how it works, we will introduce you to the different online job opportunities that you can find, we will give you advice on how to create and manage your online profile with artificial intelligence, we will show you how to improve your skills and training in this field, we will show you how to create a network of contacts and collaborators, we will help you face the challenges and risks of working online with AI.

This book is written simply and clearly, with practical and concrete examples. It is designed for those who want to start or improve their online work with AI, but also for those who are simply curious to discover the potential of this technology in the world of work.

If you're ready to make money working online, then let's get started!

Chapter 1

How to choose your market niche and your target customers

If you want to generate income working online with the use of AI, the first step is to choose your market niche and your target customers. This will allow you to focus your offer, differentiate yourself from the competition and reach the right people.

But what is a niche market? It is a specific and narrow segment of a larger market, characterized by particular needs, preferences and problems. For example, if the broad market is health and wellness, one niche might be menopausal women who want to stay fit.

And what is the customer target? This is the group of people you address with your service or product, who have the characteristics and motivations that make them potentially interested in your offer. For example, if your niche is menopausal women who want to stay in shape, your target group might be 45-55 year-old urban women who are on upper-middle income and are fitness-conscious. their health.

How can you choose your niche and your target? There are several methods and tools you can use, but here's a simple 4-step process:

Make a list of your passions, skills and experiences. This will help you identify topics and areas that you are passionate about and know well. For example, if you're passionate about photography and have experience in the industry, you might consider offering a photography-related service or product. Do **some market research.** This will help you understand if there is demand for your offering, who your competitors are, and what the market opportunities and threats are. You can use several online tools to do market research, such as Google Trends, Keyword Planner, Amazon, Udemy, Quora and others. For example, if you want to offer a service or product related to photography, you can search for what are the most searched keywords on Google related to photography, what are the best selling books and courses on Amazon and Udemy related to photography, what are the questions most frequent on Quora related to photography and so on.

Define your value proposition. This will help you communicate clearly and convincingly what you offer your customers, what benefits you bring, and why they should choose you over your competitors. You can use the following formula to define your value proposition: "I help (target) to (benefit) with (solution)."
For example, if you want to offer a photography-related service or product, your value proposition could be: "I help novice photographers improve their photos with an AI-powered online course".

Create your ideal customer profile. This will help you get to know your target customers better, understand what their demographic, psychographic and behavioral characteristics are, what their needs, wants and problems are, what their sources of information are and what their purchasing criteria are. . You can use a template called a persona to create your ideal customer profile.

A persona is a semi-fictional representation of your ideal customer based on real data and reasonable assumptions. You can use AI to create a person quickly and easily. For example, if you want to offer a service or product related to photography, your persona could be: "Marco, 35 years old, employed in a bank, lives in Milan, married with two children. He loves photography and would like to learn how to take better pictures. He has a reflex camera but doesn't know how to use it well. Look for information on the internet, on blogs and specialized sites. They want an online course that is hands-on, fun, and personalized. It has a budget of 100 euros."

By following these 4 steps, you will be able to choose your market niche and your target customers effectively and strategically. Remember that your choice is not definitive and that you can always modify or refine your niche and your target based on the feedback you receive from the market and your customers.

Chapter 2

How to create a website or blog with AI

If you want to work online, having a professional website or blog is essential to present your service or product, attract visitors and potential customers, build a reputation and trust in your sector. However, creating a website or blog isn't always easy, especially if you don't have the technical skills or time to do it. Luckily, there are AI-powered solutions that can help you create a professional website or blog quickly, easily, and effectively. In this chapter we will see what artificial intelligence is and how it can help you create a professional website or blog, what are the advantages and disadvantages of using AI for this purpose, what are the tools and platforms you can use to create your website or blog with AI and what are the best practices and tips to follow to get the best results.

What is artificial intelligence and how it can help you create a professional website or
blog Artificial intelligence is a computer science discipline that deals with creating machines capable of imitating the capabilities of human intelligence through the development of algorithms that allow you to show intelligent activity1. AI can help you create a professional website or blog in a number of ways, including by: Automatically generating your website or blog's design, layout, colors, images, fonts, and content based on your preferences, your industry, your audience, and you

- Suggesting SEO (Search Engine Optimization) best practices to optimize your website or blog for search engines and increase your visibility and organic
  traffic.

- Analyzing the data and behavior of your visitors and customers to offer you useful insights to improve your website or blog, customize your offer, increase your conversion and your loyalty.

- Creating original, relevant and quality content for your website or blog, such as text, images, videos, infographics, podcasts, etc., using natural language processing (NLP) and computer vision (CV) techniques.

  - Integrating advanced features into your website or blog, such as chatbots, virtual assistants, personalized recommendations, smart forms, etc., to make your interface more interactive, user-friendly and engaging.

Advantages and disadvantages of using AI to create a professional website or blog

Using AI to create a professional website or blog can have several benefits, including: • Save time and

money: Using AI you can create your website or blog in minutes or hours instead of days or hours. weeks, without having to hire a professional web developer or designer.

  - Have a customized website or blog: using AI you can have a website or blog that reflects your personality, your style, your brand and your specific

needs, without having to use predefined or standardized templates.

  - Have an optimized website or blog: using AI you can have a website or blog that follows the best practices of SEO, user experience (UX) and

performance, without having to do extensive research or tests and errors. • Have

an updated website or blog

- Have an updated website or blog: using AI you can have a website or blog that adapts to changes

in the market, trends, technologies and preferences of your users, without having to make manual or frequent changes .

However, using AI to build a professional website or blog can also have drawbacks, including:

- Losing control and creativity:

  using AI you can losing control and creativity on your website or blog, relying on decisions and results generated by a machine, which may not always be in line with your expectations or with your personal taste.

- Encountering limitations and technical problems: using AI you can encounter limitations and technical problems in your website or blog, such as errors, bugs, malfunctions, incompatibilities, etc., which could compromise the quality and safety of your service

- Addressing ethical and legal challenges: Using AI you can address ethical and legal challenges in your website or blog, such as respecting privacy, intellectual property, transparency, accountability, etc., which may require greater attention and caution on your part.

Tools and platforms to create your website or blog with AI

There are several tools and platforms that allow you to create your website or blog with artificial intelligence. Some examples
I am:

- **Wix ADI:** It is a feature of Wix, one of most popular platforms to create websites and blogs. Wix ADI allows you to create your website automatically and customized in minutes, answering simple questions about your industry, your goal and your preferences. You can then change the design, content and functionality of your website to your liking. Wix ADI also offers you tips to improve your SEO and UX.

- **Bookmark:** is a platform that allows you to create your website with the help of Aida, a virtual assistant based on artificial intelligence. Aida guides you step by step in creating your website, automatically generating the most suitable design, content and functions for your sector and your audience.

You can then customize your website with Bookmark's drag-and-drop editor. Aida also offers you tips for optimizing your website for search engines and mobile devices.

- **B12:** is a platform that allows you to create your website with the help of Orion, an algorithm based on artificial intelligence. Orion creates a draft of your website for you in 60 seconds, based on the information you enter about your business and needs. You can then review and approve the draft or request changes. Orion also offers you additional services such as domain management, hosting, email marketing, etc.

- **Zyro:** is a platform that allows you to create your website or blog with the help of different tools based on artificial intelligence. Zyro offers you professional and customizable templates for the design of your website or blog. Zyro also offers you tools to automatically generate the contents of your website or blog, such as texts, slogans, domain names, logos, etc. Zyro also gives you tools to analyze your website or blog data and optimize your SEO and UX.

Best practices and tips for creating a professional website or blog with AI

Creating a professional website or blog with artificial intelligence can be a quick and easy way to have an effective and quality online presence. However, there are some best practices and tips to follow to get the best results and to avoid problems or disappointments. Here are some of them:

- **Define your goal and your audience:** before To create your website or blog with AI, you need to be clear about what your goal is and what your audience is. This will help you choose the tool or platform that best suits your needs and communicate effectively and persuasively with your visitors and potential customers.

- **Choose a reliable and secure tool or platform:** Not all tools or platforms that offer the ability to create a website or blog with AI are created equal. You need to choose a tool or platform that is reliable and secure, that guarantees you the quality and functionality of your website or blog, that protects you from any technical or legal issues, that offers you good support and assistance, and that allows you to have control and ownership of your website or blog.

- **Personalize your website or blog:** Even if you use AI to create your website or blog, you don't have to just passively accept the results that are proposed to you. You need to tailor your website or blog to your personal taste, style, brand, and specific needs. You can change the design, content, functionality, etc. of your website or blog using the editors or options offered to you by the tool or platform you use.

- **Update and improve your website or blog:** Even if you use AI to build your website or blog, you don't have to abandon it once it's published. You need to update and improve your website or blog based on feedback from your users, data from your analyzes, market news, trends, technologies, etc. You can use AI tools to get suggestions or solutions to optimize your website or blog, but you must also use your critical judgment and creativity to make your website or blog unique and original.

Conclusion

In this chapter we have seen what artificial intelligence is and how it can help you create a professional website or blog, what are the advantages and disadvantages of using AI for this purpose, what are the tools and platforms you can use to create your website or blog with AI and what are the best practices and tips to follow to get the best results. We hope that this chapter has been helpful and has given you some ideas and inspiration to create your own website or blog with artificial intelligence. In the next chapter, we'll look at how to optimize your content and SEO with AI. Don't miss it!

Chapter 3

How to optimize your content and SEO with AI

If you have created your website or blog with artificial intelligence, you have taken a big step towards having a professional and quality online presence. However, this is not enough to reach your audience and potential customers. You also need to optimize your content and your SEO (Search Engine Optimization) to make your website or blog visible and relevant on search engines, especially Google. In this chapter we will see what SEO is and how it can help you optimize your content and your SEO with artificial intelligence, what are the advantages and disadvantages of using AI for this purpose, what are the tools and platforms you can use to optimize your content and your SEO with AI and what are the best practices and tips to follow to get the best results.

What is SEO and how it can help you optimize your content and SEO with AI

SEO (Search Engine Optimization) is the set of techniques and strategies that aim to increase the visibility and positioning of a website or blog among the organic (unpaid) results of a search engine, in particular of Google1.
Having a good position in the SERP (Search Engine Result Page) means having a better chance of being clicked by users looking for information, products or services related to your sector or business.

SEO is based on several factors, including:

- **The design:** it is the element that determines the aesthetic and functional aspect of your website or blog. The design must be professional, eye-catching, consistent with your brand and suitable for your audience. Furthermore, it must be responsive, i.e. adaptable to the different devices
(desktop, mobile, tablet) that users use to browse the web.

- **The technique:** it is the element that concerns the technical aspects of your website or blog. The technique must ensure the speed, security, compatibility and performance of your website or blog. In addition, it must follow
Google's guidelines to make it easier for its algorithms to crawl, index and understand your website or blog.

AI can help you optimize your content and SEO in a number of ways, including:

- Automatically generating original, relevant and quality content for your website or blog, using natural language processing (NLP) and computer vision (CV) techniques. AI can
analyze search data and identify searchers' keywords, questions, intentions, and emotions. AI can then generate content that addresses these needs in a specific
and useful way for users.

- Suggesting SEO best practices to optimize your content and SEO for search engines. AI can analyze your competitors' data and identify the winning strategies they use to rank on search engines. The AI can then suggest ways to improve your content and SEO based on these criteria.

- Analyzing the data and behavior of your users and customers to offer you useful insights to improve your content and your SEO. AI can monitor and measure the performance of your website or blog, such as traffic, conversion, retention, etc. The AI can then identify the strengths and weaknesses of your content and SEO and suggest how to optimize them based on user feedback and analytics data.

- Integrating advanced features into your website or blog, such as chatbots, virtual assistants, personalized recommendations, smart forms, etc., to make your content more interactive, user-friendly and engaging. AI can create and manage these features autonomously and intelligently, adapting to the needs and preferences of users.

Advantages and disadvantages of using AI to optimize your content and SEO

Using AI to optimize your content and SEO can have several benefits, including:

- Save time and money: using AI you can Optimize your content and SEO automatically

and quickly, without having to hire a professional SEO specialist or copywriter.

- Have a personalized content and SEO:

  using AI you can have content and SEO that adapt to your sector, your audience, your objectives and your keywords, without having to use standardized or generic solutions.

- Have optimized content and SEO: using AI

you can have content and SEO that follow Google's best user experience (UX) and performance practices, without having to do extensive research or trial and error.

- Have updated content and SEO: using AI you can have content and SEO that update according to changes in the market, trends, technologies and user preferences, without having to make manual or frequent changes.

However, using AI to optimize your content and SEO can also have drawbacks, including:

- Losing control and creativity: using AI you can losing control and creativity over your content and your SEO, relying on decisions and results generated by a machine, which may not always be in line with your expectations or with your personal taste.

- Encountering limitations and technical problems: using AI you can encounter limitations and technical problems in your content and SEO, such as errors, bugs, malfunctions, incompatibilities, etc., which could compromise the quality and safety of the your website or blog.

- Address legal and ethical challenges: Using AI you can address ethical and legal challenges in your content and SEO, such as respecting privacy, intellectual property, transparency, accountability, etc., which may require a increased attention and caution on your part.

Tools and platforms to optimize your content and yours SEO with AI

There are several tools and platforms that allow you to optimize your content and SEO with artificial intelligence. Some examples are:

- **Sentence:** it is a tool that allows you to create content optimized for SEO and for users, using natural language processing (NLP) techniques. Frase analyzes search data and identifies user questions, intentions, and emotions. Frase then helps you to create content that responds to these needs in a specific and useful way for users. Frase also offers you tips to improve your SEO and UX.

- **MarketMuse:** is a tool that allows you to optimize your content and your SEO for search engines, using natural language processing (NLP) and machine learning (ML) techniques. MarketMuse analyzes your competitors' data and identifies the winning strategies they use to position themselves on search engines. MarketMuse then suggests how to improve your content and your SEO based on these criteria. MarketMuse also offers you additional services such as content creation, content review, content management, etc.

- **RankScience:** is a tool that allows you to optimize your SEO automatically and intelligently, using machine learning (ML) techniques. RankScience monitors and measures the performance of your website or blog, such as traffic, conversion, retention, etc. RankScience then identifies the strengths and weaknesses of your SEO and suggests how to optimize them based on user feedback and analytics data. RankScience then performs A/B tests to verify the effectiveness of the proposed changes and automatically implements them if they are positive.

• **Landbot:** is a tool that allows you to integrate of advanced features in your website or blog, such as chatbots, virtual assistants, personalized recommendations, smart forms, etc., to make your content more interactive, user-friendly and engaging. Landbot creates and manages these features autonomously and intelligently, adapting to the needs and preferences of users.

Best practices and tips to optimize your content and yours SEO with AI

Optimizing your content and SEO with artificial intelligence can be a quick and easy way to increase the visibility and ranking of your website or blog on search engines.
However, there are some best practices and tips to follow to get the best results and to avoid problems or disappointments.
Here are some of them:

• Define your goal and your audience: before to optimize your content and your SEO with AI, you need to be clear about what your goal is and what your audience is. This will help you choose the tool or platform that best suits your needs and communicate effectively and persuasively with your visitors and potential customers.

• Choose a trusted and secure tool or platform: Not all tools or platforms that offer the ability to optimize your content and SEO with AI are created equal. You have to choose a tool or platform that is reliable and safe, which guarantees you the quality and functionality of yours content

• Choose a trusted and secure tool or platform: Not

all tools or platforms that offer the ability to optimize your content and SEO with AI are created equal. You need to choose a tool or platform
that is reliable and secure, that protects you from any technical or legal issues, that offers you good support and assistance, and that allows you to
have control and ownership of your content and SEO.

• Personalize your content and your SEO: Even if you use AI to optimize your content and your SEO, you don't have to just passively accept the results that
are presented to you. You need to tailor your content and SEO based on your personal taste, your style, your brand, and your specific needs. You can edit the content, meta tags, features, etc. of your website or blog using the editors or options offered to you by the tool or platform you use. • Update and improve your content and SEO: Even if you use AI to optimize your content and SEO, you don't have to abandon it once it's published. You need to update and improve your content and SEO based on feedback from your users, data from your analytics, market news, trends, technologies, etc. You can use AI tools to get suggestions or solutions to optimize your content and SEO, but you must also use your critical judgment and creativity to make your content and SEO unique and original.

Conclusion

In this chapter we have seen what SEO is and how it can help you optimize your content and your SEO with artificial intelligence, what are the advantages and disadvantages of using AI for this purpose, what are the tools and the platforms you can use to optimize your content and your SEO with AI and what are the best practices and tips to follow to get the best results. We hope this chapter has been helpful to you and has given you some ideas and inspiration to optimize your content and SEO with artificial intelligence.

Chapter 4

How to promote your service or product

If you have created and optimized your website or blog with artificial intelligence, you have taken two big steps towards having a professional and quality online presence. However, this is not enough to reach your audience and potential customers. You also need to promote your service or product with artificial intelligence, to ensure that your website or blog is known and appreciated by as many interested users as possible. In this chapter we will see what promotion with artificial intelligence is and how it can help you promote your service or product with artificial intelligence, what are the advantages and disadvantages of using AI for this purpose, which are the tools and platforms you can use to promote your service or product with and what are the best practices and advice to follow to get the best results.

What is AI promotion and how it can help you promote your service or product with AI

Promotion with artificial intelligence is the set of techniques and strategies that aim to increase the awareness and reputation of a website or blog, service or product, through the use of algorithms intelligent that allow you to show marketing activities1. Promotion with AI can help you promote your service or product in a number of ways, including:

- Automatically generating personalized and optimized advertising campaigns for your service or product, using machine learning (ML) and deep learning (DL) techniques. AI can analyze the data of your users and customers, such as their profiles, their preferences, their behaviors, their emotions, etc. The AI can then generate advertising campaigns that adapt to this data in a specific and useful way for users, choosing the channels, formats, messages, budgets, etc., that best suit your service or product.

  - Suggesting you the best marketing practices to promote your service or product with artificial intelligence. AI can analyze your competitors' data and identify the winning strategies they use to promote their services or products.

The AI can then suggest how to improve your promotion based on these criteria.

  - Analyzing the data and behavior of your users and customers to offer you useful insights to improve your promotion with artificial intelligence. AI can monitor and measure the performance of your advertising campaigns, such as traffic, conversion, retention, etc. The AI can then identify the strengths and weaknesses of your promotion and suggest how to optimize them based on user feedback and analytics data.

  - By integrating advanced features into your website or blog, such as chatbots, virtual assistants, personalized recommendations, smart forms, etc., to make your promotion more interactive, user-friendly and engaging.AI can create and manage these features autonomously and intelligently, adapting to the needs and preferences of users.

Advantages and disadvantages of using AI to promote your service or product

Using AI to promote your service or product can have several benefits, including: • Save time and money: using AI you can promote your service or your product automatically and quickly, without having to hire a marketing specialist or a professional advertiser. •

Have a personalized and optimized promotion: using AI you can have a promotion that fits your industry, your audience, your goals and your keywords, without having to use standardized or generic solutions. •

Have an updated and innovative promotion: using AI you can have a promotion that updates according to changes in the market, trends, technologies and user preferences, without having to make manual or frequent changes. Furthermore, you can have a promotion that takes advantage of the most advanced and modern features of the web, such as chatbots, virtual assistants, personalized recommendations, intelligent forms, etc.

However, using AI to promote your service or product can also have disadvantages, including: • Losing control and creativity: Using AI you can lose control and creativity over your promotion, relying on decisions and results generated by a machine, which may not always be in line with your expectations or your personal taste. •

Encountering limitations and technical problems: using AI you can encounter limitations and technical problems in your promotion, such as errors, bugs, malfunctions, incompatibilities, etc., which could compromise the quality and safety of your service

• Addressing ethical and legal challenges: Using AI you can address ethical and legal challenges in your promotion, such as respecting privacy, intellectual property, transparency, accountability, etc., which may require greater attention and caution from you.

Tools and platforms to promote your service or product with AI

There are several tools and platforms that allow you to promote your service or product with artificial intelligence. Some examples are: • **Google**

Ads: is a tool that allows you to create personalized and optimized advertising campaigns for your service or product, using machine learning (ML) and deep learning (DL) techniques. Google Ads analyzes the data of your users and customers, such as their profiles, their preferences, their behaviour, their emotions, etc. Google Ads then helps you create advertising campaigns that adapt to this data in a specific and useful way for users, choosing channels (such as Google search, YouTube, Gmail, Google Ads then helps you create advertising campaigns that adapt to this data in a specific and useful way for users, choosing channels (such as Google search, YouTube, Gmail, Google Display Network, etc.), formats (such as text, image, video, etc.), messages, budget, etc., best suited to your serv Google Ads also offers you suggestions to improve your advertising campaigns based on analytics data and performance.

• **Mailchimp:** is a tool that allows you to create personalized and optimized email marketing campaigns for your service or product, using machine learning (ML) and natural language processing (NLP) techniques. Mailchimp analyzes the data of your users and customers, such as their profiles, their preferences, their behaviors, their emotions, etc.

Mailchimp then helps you create email marketing campaigns that adapt to this data in a specific and useful way for users, choosing the most suitable templates, contents, subjects, calls to action, sending times, etc. to your service or product. Mailchimp also offers you suggestions to improve your email marketing campaigns based on analytics data and performance.

- **Landbot:** is a tool that allows you to integrate advanced features in your website or blog, such as chatbots, virtual assistants, personalized recommendations, smart forms, etc., to make your promotion more interactive, user-friendly and engaging. Landbot creates and manages these features autonomously and intelligently, adapting to the needs and preferences of users.

Good practices and tips to promote your service or product with AI

Promoting your service or product with artificial intelligence can be a quick and easy way to increase the awareness and reputation of your website or blog, your service or your product. However, there are some best practices and tips to follow to get the best results and to avoid problems or disappointments. Here are some of them:

- Define your goal and your audience: Before promoting your service or product with AI, you need to be clear on what your goal is and what your audience is. This will help you choose the tool or platform that best suits your needs and communicate effectively and persuasively with your visitors and potential customers.

- Choose a reliable and secure tool or platform: Not all tools or platforms that offer the possibility to promote your service or product with AI are the same. You need to choose a tool or platform that is reliable and secure, that protects you from anytechnical or legal issues, that offers you good support and assistance, and that allows you to have control and ownership of your promotion.

- Customize your promotion: even if you use AI to promote your service or product, you don't have to just passively accept the results that are offered

to you. You need to tailor your promotion to your personal taste, your style, your brand and your specific needs. You can modify the advertising campaigns, email marketing, features, etc. of your website or blog using the editors or options offered to you by the tool or platform you use.

- Update and improve your promotion: Even if you use AI to promote your service or product, you don't have to abandon it once it's published. You need to update and improve your promotion based on feedback from your users, data from your analyzes, market news, trends, technologies, etc. You can use AI tools

to get suggestions or solutions to optimize your promotion, but you must also use your critical judgment and creativity to make your promotion unique and original.

Conclusion

In this chapter we have seen what promotion with artificial intelligence is and how it can help you promote your service or product with artificial intelligence, what are the advantages and disadvantages of using AI for this purpose, what are the tools and platforms you can use to promote your service or product with AI and what are the best practices and advice to follow to get the best results. We hope this chapter has been helpful to you and has given you some ideas and inspiration to promote your service or product with AI. In the next chapter we will look at how to measure the success of your website or blog with AI. Don't miss it!

Chapter 5

How to measure the success of your website or blog

If you have created, optimized and promoted your website or blog
with artificial intelligence, you have taken three big steps
towards having a professional and quality online presence. However,
this is not enough to reach your audience and potential customers.
You also need to measure the success of your website or
blog with artificial intelligence, to ensure that your website or
blog is effective and performing on search engines and in the
market. In this chapter we will see what AI measurement is and how
it can help you measure the success of your website or blog with
AI, what are the advantages and disadvantages of using AI for this
purpose, what are the tools and platforms you can use to measure
the success of your website or blog with AI and what are the best
practices and tips to follow to get the best results.

**What is AI measurement and how it can help you measure
the success of your website or blog with AI**

Measurement with artificial intelligence is the set of techniques
and strategies that have the purpose of collecting, analyzing
and interpreting data from the web in order to understand
and optimize the behavior of visitors to your website or blog, your
your service or product.
Measuring with AI can help you measure the success of your
website or blog in a number of ways, including:

- Generating reports and dashboards automatically
  customized and optimized for your website or blog,
  using machine learning (ML) and natural language
  processing (NLP) techniques. AI can analyze data
  coming from your website or blog, such as traffic,
  conversion, retention, etc. The AI can then
  generate reports and dashboards that clearly and
  simply show you the most relevant metrics and
  indicators for your website or blog, choosing the formats,
  graphics, texts, etc., that best suit your goal .

Suggesting web analytics best practices to measure the success of your website or blog with artificial intelligence. AI can analyze your competitors' data and identify the winning strategies they use to measure the success of their websites or blogs. The AI can then suggest ways to improve your measurement based on these criteria.

- Analyzing the data and behavior of your visitors to offer you useful insights to improve the success of your website or blog with artificial intelligence. AI can monitor and measure the performance of your website or blog, such as traffic, conversion, retention, etc. The AI can then identify the strengths and weaknesses of your website or blog and suggest how to optimize them based on visitor feedback and analytics data.

- Integrating advanced features into your website or blog, such as chatbots, virtual assistants, personalized recommendations, smart forms, etc., to make your measurement more interactive, user-friendly and engaging. AI can create and manage these features autonomously and intelligently, adapting to the needs and preferences of visitors.

Pros and cons of using AI to measure the success of your website or blog

Using AI to measure the success of your website or blog can have several benefits, including:

- Save time and money: using AI you can measure the success of your website or blog automatically and quickly, without having to hire a professional web analytics specialist or data analyst.

- Have a personalized and optimized measurement: using AI you can have a measurement that adapts to your industry, your audience, your goal and your metrics, without having to use standardized or generic solutions. • Have

an updated and innovative measurement: using AI you can have a measurement that updates according to changes in the market, trends, technologies and visitor preferences, without having to make manual or frequent changes. Furthermore, you can have a measurement that takes advantage of the most advanced and modern features of the web, such as chatbots, virtual assistants, personalized recommendations, intelligent forms, etc.

However, using AI to measure the success of your website or blog can also have disadvantages, including: • Losing control and creativity: Using AI you can lose control

control and creativity over your measurement, relying on decisions and results generated by a machine, which may not always be in line with your expectations or your personal taste. • Encountering limitations

and technical problems: Using AI you can encounter limitations and technical problems in your measurement, such as errors, bugs, malfunctions, incompatibilities, etc., which could compromise the quality and security of your website or blog.

- Facing ethical and legal challenges in your own measurement, such as compliance with privacy, intellectual property, transparency, accountability, etc., which may require greater attention and caution on your part.

Tools and platforms to measure the success of your website or blog with AI

There are several tools and platforms that allow you to measure the success of your website or blog with artificial intelligence. Some examples are: • **Google Analytics:** is a tool that allows you to collect, analyze and interpret data from your website or blog, using machine learning (ML) and natural language processing (NLP) techniques. Google Analytics offers you customized and optimized reports and dashboards for your website or blog, which clearly and easily show you the most relevant metrics and indicators for your website or blog. Google Analytics also offers you suggestions to improve your website or blog based on analytics data and performance.

• **Semrush:** is a tool that allows you to monitor and optimize the SEO performance of your website or blog, using machine learning (ML) and natural language processing (NLP) techniques. Semrush offers you customized and optimized reports and dashboards for your website or blog, which clearly and easily show you the most relevant metrics and indicators for your website or blog in terms of search engine rankings, organic traffic , keywords, backlinks, etc. Semrush also offers you suggestions to improve your website or blog based on analytics data and performance.

• **Landbot:** is a tool that allows you to integrate of advanced features in your website or blog, such as chatbots, virtual assistants, personalized recommendations, smart forms, etc., to make your measurement more interactive, user-friendly and engaging. Landbot creates and manages these features autonomously and intelligently, adapting to the needs and preferences of visitors.

Best practices and tips for measuring the success of your website or blog with AI

Measuring the success of your website or blog with artificial intelligence can be a quick and easy way to have a quality, professional online presence. However, there are some best practices and tips to follow to get the best results and to avoid problems or disappointments. Here are some of them:

• Define your goal and metrics: Before To measure the success of your website or blog with AI, you need to be clear about what your goal is and what your metrics are. This will help you choose the tool or platform that best suits your needs and correctly and usefully interpret the data you are provided with. Not all data is equally important for your website or blog, you need to select the ones that are most relevant to your goal and that allow you to evaluate the success of your website or blog.

• Choose a reliable and secure tool or platform: Not all tools or platforms that offer the ability to measure the success of your website or blog with AI are created equal. You need to choose a tool or platform that is reliable and secure, that protects you from any technical or legal issues, that offers you good support and assistance, and that allows you to have control and ownership of your data.

• Customize your measurement: Even if you use AI to measure the success of your website or blog, you don't have to just passively accept the results that are presented to you. You need to tailor your measurement to your personal taste, your style, your brand, and your specific needs. You can modify the reports and dashboards, features, etc. of your website or blog using the editors or options that are offered to you by the tool or platform you use.

- Update and improve your measurement: Even if you use AI to measure the success of your website or blog, you don't have to abandon it once you get the data. You need to update and improve your measurement based on feedback from your visitors, data from your analytics, market news, trends, technologies, etc. You can use AI tools to get suggestions or solutions to optimize your measurement, but you must also use your critical judgment and creativity to make your measurement unique and original.

Conclusion

In this chapter we have seen what AI measurement is and how it can help you measure the success of your website or blog with AI, what are the advantages and disadvantages of using AI for this purpose , what tools and platforms you can use to measure the success of your website or blog with AI and what are the best practices and tips to follow to get the best results. We hope that this chapter has been helpful and has given you some ideas and inspiration for measuring the success of your website or blog with artificial intelligence.

Chapter 6

How to automate your activities and your processes

If you've built, optimized, promoted, and measured the success of your website or blog with artificial intelligence, you've taken four big steps towards having a quality, professional online presence.

However, this is not enough to reach your audience and potential customers. You also need to automate your tasks and processes with artificial intelligence, to make your website or blog efficient and scalable in the market. In this chapter we will see what automation with artificial intelligence is and how it can help you automate your tasks and processes with artificial intelligence, what are the advantages and disadvantages of using AI for this purpose, which are the tools and platforms you can use to automate your activities and processes with AI and what are the best practices and advice to follow to get the best results.

What is automation with artificial intelligence and how it can help you automate your tasks and processes with AI

Automation with artificial intelligence is the set of techniques and strategies that aim to automatically and intelligently carry out activities and processes that require human intervention, using intelligent algorithms that mimic the behavior of operators1. Automation with AI can help you automate your tasks and processes in a number of ways, including:

- Automatically generating customized and optimized software robots (or bots) for your activities and processes, using machine learning (ML) and natural language processing (NLP) techniques. AI can analyze your activities and processes, such as data management, customer communication, content creation, etc. The AI can then generate robot software that automatically and intelligently executes your activities and processes, interacting with computer applications exactly as you would.

- Suggesting the best automation practices for your activities and processes with artificial intelligence. AI can analyze your activities and processes and identify automation opportunities that can bring you benefits in terms of time, money, quality, etc. The AI can then suggest ways to improve your automation based on these criteria.

- Analyzing the data and behavior of your software robots to offer you useful insights to improve your automation with artificial intelligence. AI can monitor and measure the performance of your robot software, such as speed, accuracy, security, etc.
The AI can then identify the strengths and weaknesses of your automation and suggest how to optimize them based on feedback from the software robots and analytics data.

Advantages and disadvantages of using AI to automate your tasks and processes

Using artificial intelligence to automate your tasks and processes can have several benefits, including:

- Save time and money: using AI you can automate your activities and processes in an automatic and intelligent way, without having to hire or train human operators or without having to manually perform repetitive and tedious operations.

- Increase quality and safety: using AI you can automate your activities and processes accurately and reliably, reducing errors, risks, frauds, data losses, etc., which could result from an intervention human.

- Scaling your business: using AI you can automate your activities and processes in a flexible and adaptable way, increasing your ability to manage a greater number of customers, data, requests, etc., without having to invest in new resources or infrastructure.

However, using artificial intelligence to automate your activities and processes can also have disadvantages, including: • Losing control and creativity: using AI you can lose control and creativity over your activities and processes, relying on decisions and results generated by a machine, which may not always be in line with your expectations or with your personal taste.

• Encountering limitations and technical problems: using AI you can encounter limitations and technical problems in your automation, such as errors, bugs, malfunctions, incompatibilities, etc., which could compromise the quality and safety of your activities and your processes.

• Facing ethical and legal challenges in your own automation, such as respecting privacy, intellectual property, transparency, accountability, etc., which may require greater attention and caution on your part.

Tools and platforms to automate your activities and processes with AI

There are several tools and platforms that allow you to automate your activities and processes with artificial intelligence. Some examples are:

• **Power Automate:** is a tool that allows you to create and manage automated workflows for your activities and processes, using machine learning (ML) and natural language processing (NLP) techniques. Power Automate offers you a wide range of templates and connectors to create customized and optimized workflows for your activities and processes, which integrate with the computer applications you use every day, such as Office 365, Dynamics 365, SharePoint, etc. Power Automate also offers you the ability to create robot software to automate your tasks and processes on your local computer.

- **UiPath:** is a tool that allows you to create e manage robot software customized and optimized for your activities and processes, using machine learning (ML) and natural language processing (NLP) techniques. UiPath offers you a complete platform for creating robot software that automatically and intelligently executes your activities and processes, interacting with computer applications exactly as you would. UiPath also offers you the possibility to monitor and analyze the performance of your robot software thanks to dashboards and reports.

- **Zapier:** is a tool that allows you to create and manage simple and fast automations for your activities and processes, using machine learning (ML) and natural language processing (NLP) techniques. Zapier offers you a wide range of connectors to create personalized and optimized automations for your tasks and processes, which integrate with the computer applications you use every day, such as Gmail, Slack, Dropbox, etc. Zapier also offers you the possibility to create custom automations using the Python or Javascript language.

Best practices and tips to automate your activities and processes with AI

Automating your tasks and processes with artificial intelligence can be a quick and easy way to increase your efficiency and your scalability in the market. However, there are some best practices and tips to follow to get the best results and to avoid problems or disappointments. Here are some of them:

- Define your goal and your use cases: Before automating your activities and processes with AI, you need to be clear on what your goal is and what your use cases are. This will help you choose the tool or platform that best suits your needs and create robot software or automations that are effective and useful for your activities and processes.

- Choose a trusted and secure tool or platform: Not all tools or platforms that offer the ability to automate your tasks and processes with AI are created equal. You need to choose a tool or platform that is reliable and secure, that protects you from any technical or legal issues, that offers you good support and assistance, and that allows you to have control and ownership of your robot software or automations .

- Test and monitor your automation: before launching your automation with AI, you must test it and verify its functioning, accuracy, safety, etc., to avoid errors, bugs, malfunctions, incompatibilities, etc., which they could harm your business and your processes. Furthermore, you need to monitor your automation with AI, to check its performance, results, feedback,

etc., to evaluate the success of your automation and to make any improvements or changes.

Conclusion

In this chapter we have seen what automation with artificial intelligence is and how it can help you automate your tasks and processes with artificial intelligence, what are the advantages and disadvantages of using AI for this purpose, what are the tools and platforms you can use to automate your activities and processes with AI and what are the best practices and advice to follow to get the best results. We hope that this chapter has been useful to you and has given you some ideas and inspiration to automate your tasks and processes with artificial intelligence.

Chapter 7

How to improve your skills and training with AI

Working online is an opportunity that offers many benefits, but also some challenges. One of these is to keep one's skills and training up-to-date, in an industry that changes rapidly and requires constant adaptability. So how do you improve your skills and remain competitive in the online job market? In this chapter, we will show you how artificial intelligence (AI) can be a valuable ally for your professional development.

AI is the science and technology that deals with creating systems capable of performing tasks that normally require human intelligence, such as image recognition, natural language understanding, problem solving, machine learning, and so on . AI is already present in many areas of our daily lives, such as smartphone apps, search engines, social media, streaming services, smart devices and much more. AI can also help you improve your skills and education in several ways:

- It can help you to identify your weaknesses and your strengths. There are several online platforms that offer AI-based tests and assessments, which allow you to measure your proficiency level in various fields, such as foreign languages, digital skills, soft skills, and so on. These quizzes give you personalized feedback and suggest areas you need to work on more and areas you're already good at. This way, you can focus your attention on the skills most relevant to your career goal.

- It can help you find the resources that best suit your needs. The web is full of free or low-cost resources for learning new skills or deepening existing ones. However, it is not always easy to choose the ones that best suit your level, your learning style and your interests. Thankfully, there are several AI-powered tools that help you select the most appropriate resources for you. For example, there are smart search engines that show you the most relevant online courses based on your preferences and goals. Or there are apps that offer you personalized content based on your profile and your progress.

- It can help you make your learning more effective and efficient. AI can also support you throughout the learning process, providing you with features that help you better retain information, better understand concepts, better solve problems, and better verify your results. For example, there are apps that use AI to create smart flashcards that adjust to your pace and forgetfulness curve. Or there are systems that use AI to generate questions and answers based on the content you are studying. Or there are virtual tutors who use AI to give you real-time suggestions and feedback.

• It can help you certify your ea skills
value them on the market. Finally, AI can also help
you demonstrate your skills and make them visible to
potential employers or clients. In fact, there are
several online platforms that offer AI-based
certifications, which certify your level of competence in
various fields in various sectors, such as foreign
languages, digital skills, soft skills and so on.
These certifications are internationally
recognized and can be incorporated into your
resume or online profile.
Furthermore, there are services that use AI to create
digital portfolios, which collect and display your
projects, your work and your references in a
professional and captivating way.

As you can see, AI can be a great ally for your online professional
development. However, to make the most of its potential,
you must also be aware of its limitations and risks. AI is not infallible
and can make mistakes or bias. AI is no substitute for your critical
judgment and creativity. AI cannot guarantee success if you are
not motivated and committed. For this, we advise you to use AI as
a complementary tool and not as a magic solution. Use AI to
enrich your learning, not flatten it. Use AI to expand your
opportunities, not limit them.

Conclusion

In this chapter, we've shown you how AI can help you improve
your online skills and education. We've introduced you to some
examples of AI-powered platforms and tools you can use to
assess, find, learn, and certify your skills. We've also given you
some tips on how to use AI responsibly and effectively. We hope
you found this information useful and encourage you to
experiment with AI in your online career path.

Chapter 8

How to create a network of contacts and collaborators

Working online doesn't mean working alone. Indeed, to be successful in online work, it is essential to create and maintain a network of contacts and collaborators who can offer you support, advice, opportunities and feedback. However, building and managing an online network isn't always easy. How, then, to build and consolidate your professional relationships online? In this chapter, we'll show you how artificial intelligence (AI) can be a valuable ally for your online networking.

AI is the science and technology that deals with creating systems capable of performing tasks that normally require human intelligence, such as image recognition, natural language understanding, problem solving, machine learning, and so on . AI is already present in many areas of our daily lives, such as smartphone apps, search engines, social media, streaming services, smart devices and much more.

AI can also help you build and manage your online network in several ways:

- It can help you identify the people best suited to your professional goal. There are several online platforms that use AI to analyze your profile, your industry, your interests and your goals and suggest the most compatible people for you. These people can be potential employers, clients, partners, mentors or simply people to share experiences and ideas with. These platforms also allow you to get in touch with these people simply and directly, by sending them personalized messages or participating in chats or video calls.

• It can help you keep in touch with people of your network. AI can also support you in keeping alive the relationship with the people you've met online, offering you features that help you communicate effectively and empathetically. For example, there are apps that use AI to create smart reminders, reminding you when to contact someone in your network or when to reply to a message. Or there are systems that use AI to generate interesting and relevant content to share with your network, such as articles, videos or podcasts.

• It can help you collaborate with people in your network. AI can also make it easier for you to work together with people in your network on joint projects, providing features that help you coordinate tasks, manage documents, resolve conflicts and evaluate results. For example, there are platforms that use AI to create shared calendars that adapt to the availability and preferences of each participant. Or there are services that use AI to create collaborative documents, which update in real time and integrate different sources of information. Or there is software that uses AI to detect and resolve conflicts between team members, proposing solutions and compromises. Or there are systems that use AI to evaluate the quality and impact of the projects carried out, providing feedback and suggestions.

As you can see, AI can be a great ally for your online networking. However, to make the most of its potential, you must also be aware of its limitations and risks. AI is not infallible and can make mistakes or bias. AI cannot replace your human relationship and trust with people.
AI cannot guarantee your success if you are not proactive and collaborative. For this, we advise you to use AI as a complementary tool and not as a magic solution. Use AI to enrich your networking, not flatten it. Use AI to broaden your relationships, not limit them.

Conclusion

In this chapter, we've shown you how AI can help you build and manage your online network. We've introduced you to a few examples of AI-powered platforms and tools you can use to identify, contact, communicate, and collaborate with the people who are best suited to your career goal. We've also given you some tips on how to use AI responsibly and effectively.
We hope you found this information helpful and

encourage you to experiment with AI in your online networking journey.

Chapter 9

How to deal with the challenges and risks of working online

Working online is an opportunity that offers many benefits, but also some challenges and risks. One of these is to manage your online security and privacy, in a context that can be exposed to various threats, such as data theft, scams, viruses, hackers and so on. Another challenge is maintaining one's physical and mental well-being online, in an environment that can be stressful, isolating, destructive and alienating. So how do you protect your integrity and health online? In this chapter, we'll show you how artificial intelligence (AI) can be a valuable ally for your online work.

AI is the science and technology that deals with creating systems capable of performing tasks that normally require human intelligence, such as image recognition, natural language understanding, problem solving, machine learning, and so on . AI is already present in many areas of our daily lives, such as smartphone apps, search engines, social media, streaming services, smart devices and much more.

AI can also help you deal with the challenges and risks of working online in several ways:

• It can help you protect your data and privacy online. There are several online platforms and tools that use AI to ensure the safety and confidentiality of your personal and professional data online. For example, there are services that use AI to encrypt your data and make it unreadable to anyone who doesn't have the access keys. Or there is software that uses AI to detect and block possible online threats, such as viruses, hackers or scams. Or there are apps that use AI to monitor and limit access to your data by third parties, such as companies or governments.

Let's take some examples:

- **Signal** is a messaging and calling service that uses AI to encrypt your data and make it unreadable to anyone without access keys. This way, you can communicate securely and privately with people in your online network, without the risk of your messages or calls being intercepted or snooped on by someone.

- **Norton** is security software that uses AI to detect and block possible online threats, such as viruses, hackers or scams. This way, you can surf the web safely and peacefully, without the risk of your computer or devices being infected or compromised by someone.

- **Jumbo** is an app that uses AI to monitor and restrict access to your data by third parties, such as companies or governments. In this way, you can control and manage your online privacy, without the risk of your data being collected or used by someone without your consent.

- **It can help you maintain your physical and mental well-being online.** There are several online platforms and tools that use AI to promote your health and balance online. For example:

  - **Headspace** is a meditation and mindfulness service that uses AI to create personalized sessions based on your needs and goals. In this way, you can reduce stress and anxiety, improve concentration and creativity, increase happiness and gratitude.

  - **Fitbit** is a smart device that uses AI to track your physical activity and sleep. This way, you can keep track of your progress and results, receive advice and feedback, set goals and challenges.

- **Woebot** is a chatbot that uses AI to offer you a psychological support. This way, you can talk to a virtual friend who listens to you, understands you, encourages you and helps you manage your emotions and problems.

As you can see, AI can be a great ally for your online work. However, to make the most of its potential, you must also be aware of its limitations and risks. AI is not infallible and can make mistakes or bias; it can't replace your sense of responsibility and caution online. It cannot guarantee your well-being if you are not observant and curious online. For this, we advise you to use it as a
complementary tool and not as a magic solution. Use AI to protect your work online, not expose it. Use this technology to improve your online well-being, not to undermine it.

In conclusion, in this chapter we have shown you how Artificial Intelligence can help you deal with the challenges and risks of working online. We have introduced you to some examples of AI-powered platforms and tools that you can use to protect your data and privacy online, to maintain your physical and mental well-being online. We've also given you some tips on how to use this technology responsibly and effectively. We hope you found this information useful and encourage you to experiment with AI in your online work.

CONCLUSIONS

In this book we have shown you how to earn money by working online, exploiting the potential of artificial intelligence (AI). We have explained what it is and how it works, we have introduced you to the different online job opportunities that you can find thanks to AI, we have given you advice on how to create and manage your online profile, showing you how to improve your skills and your training with AI. Showing you how to create a network of contacts and collaborators with

this modern tool, thus helping you to face the challenges and risks of working online.

We hope you found this book helpful and inspired you to embark on your journey to working online with AI. However, our work doesn't end there. To be successful in online work, you also need to be able to evaluate your achievements and goals with AI. You must be able to measure your impact and satisfaction in online work, recognize your strengths and areas for improvement, update your goals and strategies based on market changes and your needs .

To do this, in fact, there are several online platforms and tools that use AI to help you evaluate your results and your goals, such as: • **Google Analytics** is a

service that uses AI to

analyze the traffic and conversions of your website or blog.

In this way, you can understand how many visitors you have, where they come from, what they do on your site, how much time they spend there, which pages are most viewed and which actions are most performed.

• **LinkedIn** is a platform that uses AI to analyze your professional profile and your network. In this way, you can understand how visible and sought after you are in the online job

market, which skills are most in demand and most appreciated, which people are the most influential and most useful for your professional goal.

- **Reflectly** is an app that uses AI to create an intelligent personal journal. In this way, you can reflect on your experiences and emotions in working online, receive personalized feedback and advice, set goals and action plans.

These are just a few examples of platforms and tools you can use to evaluate your results and goals. We invite you to also discover and experiment with other tools that may suit your needs and preferences.

Remember that working online is a dynamic and ongoing process, requiring constant attention and constant adaptability.
AI can be a great ally for your online work, but it can't replace your will, your passion and your creativity. Use it as a tool to facilitate your online work, but never forget your human worth and sense of purpose.

Thanks for reading this book.

We wish you a good start on this wonderful journey.

*Crafty Ink **Manolo***